36 INSPIRATIONAL & MOTIVATIONAL QUOTES TO LIVE BY

Daily Wisdom to Inspire Personal Growth, Resilience, Positivity, and Mindfulness

Prosper Press

This Book Belongs To:

_____

Contents

Introduction

Welcome to "365 Inspirational & Motivational Quotes to Live By," a curated collection of wisdom designed to uplift your spirit, guide your journey, and illuminate each day with hope and insight. Life is an ever-evolving tapestry of experiences, and within these pages, you will find the threads of inspiration needed to weave your own beautiful narrative.

In this book, you will encounter quotes that speak to the heart of human experience—our triumphs, our struggles, and our relentless pursuit of growth and understanding. Each chapter is dedicated to a different facet of life, offering perspectives that are as diverse as they are profound. This is not just a book to be read but a companion to be revisited whenever you seek guidance or a spark of inspiration.

Chapter 1: Adversity, Resilience, and Strength - Life's challenges can be daunting, but they also shape our strength and character. In this chapter, you'll find quotes that remind you of your innate resilience and capacity to rise above adversity.

Chapter 2: Personal Growth and Self Improvement - The journey of self-improvement is a lifelong endeavor. This chapter provides quotes that inspire you to reach for your highest potential and embrace the continuous process of becoming your best self.

Chapter 3: Education and Learning - Knowledge is a powerful tool for transformation. Here, you'll discover quotes that celebrate the joy of learning and the boundless opportunities it brings.

Chapter 4: Self-Love and Acceptance - True fulfillment begins with self-acceptance. These quotes encourage you to embrace your unique qualities and cultivate a deep sense of self-love.

Chapter 5: Positivity, Gratitude, and Joy - A positive outlook can transform your life. This chapter offers quotes that inspire gratitude, joy, and a bright perspective on the world around you.

Chapter 6: Creativity and Innovation - Innovation drives progress and creativity fuels our dreams. In this chapter, you'll find quotes that encourage you to think outside the box and bring your imaginative ideas to life.

Chapter 7: Goal Setting, Achievement, and Success - Achieving your dreams requires clarity, dedication, and hard work. These quotes provide motivation and guidance to help you set and accomplish your goals.

Chapter 8: Empathy and Kindness - Compassion and understanding are the cornerstones of a harmonious world. This chapter is filled with quotes that highlight the importance of empathy and the transformative power of kindness.

Chapter 9: Relationships and Community - Human connections enrich our lives in countless ways. Here, you'll find quotes that celebrate the beauty of relationships and the strength of community.

Chapter 10: Teamwork and Collaboration - Great achievements are rarely the work of one individual. These quotes emphasize the importance of working together and the synergy that arises from collaboration.

Chapter 11: Mindfulness and Inner Peace - Inner peace is the foundation of a balanced life. This chapter offers quotes that guide you towards mindfulness and a deeper sense of tranquility.

As you journey through this book, may these quotes serve as beacons of light, guiding you through the complexities of life with wisdom and grace. Each day brings new challenges and opportunities, and within these pages, you'll find the inspiration to navigate them with resilience, joy, and a compassionate heart. Remember, you are never alone on this journey—these words, and the wisdom they carry, are here to support you every step of the way.

Chapter 1

Adversity, Resilience, and Strength

Welcome to Chapter 1, where we dive into the powerful themes of overcoming adversity and developing resilience. As we embark on this journey, it's important to recognize that the challenges we face are not just obstacles to be endured, but opportunities for growth and transformation. This chapter sets the stage for the rest of the book, highlighting the strength and perseverance that emerge from facing life's toughest trials head-on.

Consider the life of **Nelson Mandela**, who endured 27 years of imprisonment during his struggle against apartheid in South Africa. Despite the harsh conditions and prolonged separation from his loved ones, Mandela's resilience never wavered. His ability to transform personal suffering into a broader movement for justice and equality is a testament to the indomitable human spirit. Mandela's quote, reminds us that resilience is built through unwavering hope and steadfast determination.

Another inspiring example is **Helen Keller**, who lost her sight and hearing at a very young age. With the guidance of her dedicated teacher, Anne Sullivan, Keller learned to communicate and went on to become an influential author, activist, and lecturer. Her life story is a powerful reminder that resilience and the desire to overcome adversity can lead to extraordinary achievements. Keller's words,

> Although the world is full of suffering, it is also full of the overcoming of it.

encourage us to find strength in our struggles and to persist in the face of seemingly insurmountable odds.

In this chapter, you will encounter quotes that not only inspire resilience but also provide practical wisdom for navigating life's challenges. Let these words serve as a beacon of hope, reminding you that every obstacle is an opportunity to grow stronger, wiser, and more resilient. Embrace the lessons of adversity, and allow them to fuel your journey toward a brighter, more resilient future.

Quote #1

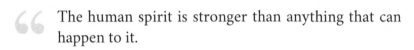

The human spirit is stronger than anything that can happen to it.

— C.C. Scott

Quote #2

Adversity has the effect of eliciting talents, which in prosperous circumstances would have lain dormant.

— Horace

Quote #3

It's not whether you get knocked down, it's whether you get up.

— Vince Lombardi

Quote #4

We don't develop courage by being happy every day. We develop it by surviving difficult times and challenging adversity.

— Barbara De Angelis

Quote #5

You may have to fight a battle more than once to win it.

— Margaret Thatcher

Quote #6

Hard times don't create heroes. It is during the hard times when the 'hero' within us is revealed.

— Bob Riley

Quote #7

Turn your wounds into wisdom.

— Oprah Winfrey

Quote #8

The gem cannot be polished without friction, nor man perfected without trials.

— Chinese Proverb

QUOTE #9

Rock bottom became the solid foundation on which I rebuilt my life.

— J.K. Rowling

QUOTE #10

Difficulties are meant to rouse, not discourage. The human spirit is to grow strong by conflict.

— William Ellery Channing

QUOTE #11

Only those who dare to fail greatly can ever achieve greatly.

— Robert F. Kennedy

QUOTE #12

Adversity is another way to measure the greatness of individuals. I never had a crisis that didn't make me stronger.

— Lou Holtz

QUOTE #13

“ When you come to the end of your rope, tie a knot and hang on.

— Franklin D. Roosevelt

QUOTE #14

“ There is no better than adversity. Every defeat, every heartbreak, every loss, contains its own seed, its own lesson on how to improve your performance the next time.

— Malcolm X

QUOTE #15

“ He who overcomes others is strong; He who overcomes himself is mighty.

— Lao Tzu

QUOTE #16

“ It is under the greatest adversity that there exists the greatest potential for doing good, both for oneself and others.

— Dalai Lama

Quote #17

" Adversity causes some men to break; others to break records.

— William Arthur Ward

Quote #18

" The art of living lies less in eliminating our troubles than in growing with them.

— Bernard Baruch

Quote #19

" I ask not for a lighter burden, but for broader shoulders.

— Jewish Proverb

Quote #20

" Every adversity, every failure, every heartache carries with it the seed of an equal or greater benefit.

— Napoleon Hill

Quote #21

" Fire is the test of gold; adversity, of strong men.

— Martha Graham

Quote #22

"" Strength does not come from winning. Your struggles develop your strengths.

— Arnold Schwarzenegger

Quote #23

"" You'll never find a better sparring partner than adversity.

— Golda Meir

Quote #24

"" Adversity is like a strong wind. It tears away from us all but the things that cannot be torn, so that we see ourselves as we really are.

— Arthur Golden

Quote #25

"" Problems are not stop signs, they are guidelines.

— Robert H. Schuller

Quote #26

"" The oak fought the wind and was broken, the willow bent when it must and survived.

— Robert Jordan

Quote #27

" It does not matter how slowly you go as long as you do not stop.

— Confucius

Quote #28

" Show me someone who has done something worthwhile, and I'll show you someone who has overcome adversity.

— Lou Holtz

Quote #29

" What does not kill us makes us stronger.

— Friedrich Nietzsche

Quote #30

" In times of great stress or adversity, it's always best to keep busy, to plow your anger and your energy into something positive.

— Lee Iacocca

Quote #31

❝ The greatest oak was once a little nut who held its ground.

— Unknown

Quote #32

❝ Grit is that 'extra something' that separates the most successful people from the rest. It's the passion, perseverance, and stamina that we must channel to stick with our dreams until they become a reality.

— Travis Bradberry

Quote #33

❝ Resilience is when you address uncertainty with flexibility.

— Anonymous

Quote #34

❝ Success is not final, failure is not fatal: It is the courage to continue that counts.

— Winston Churchill

Quote #35

66 The human capacity for burden is like bamboo – far more flexible than you'd ever believe at first glance.

— Jodi Picoult

Quote #36

66 A hero is an ordinary individual who finds the strength to persevere and endure in spite of overwhelming obstacles.

— Christopher Reeve

Quote #37

66 Our greatest glory is not in never falling, but in rising every time we fall.

— Confucius

Quote #38

66 Resilience is knowing that you are the only one that has the power and the responsibility to pick yourself up.

— Mary Holloway

Quote #39

❝ I am not afraid of storms, for I am learning how to sail my ship.

— Louisa May Alcott

Quote #40

❝ It is really wonderful how much resilience there is in human nature. Let any obstructing cause, no matter what, be removed in any way, even by death, and we fly back to first principles of hope and enjoyment.

— Bram Stoker

Quote #41

❝ Life doesn't get easier or more forgiving, we get stronger and more resilient.

— Steve Maraboli

Quote #42

❝ You don't drown by falling in the water; you drown by staying there.

— Edwin Louis Cole

Quote #43

❝ Persistence and resilience only come from having been given the chance to work through difficult problems.

— Gever Tulley

Quote #44

❝ Courage doesn't always roar. Sometimes courage is the quiet voice at the end of the day saying, 'I will try again tomorrow.'

— Mary Anne Radmacher

Quote #45

❝ Resilience is not what happens to you. It's how you react to, respond to, and recover from what happens to you.

— Jeffrey Gitomer

Quote #46

❝ Endurance is not just the ability to bear a hard thing, but to turn it into glory.

— William Barclay

Quote #47

66 Be like the cliff against which the waves continually break; but it stands firm and tames the fury of the water around it.

— Marcus Aurelius

Quote #48

66 Life is not about how fast you run or how high you climb, but how well you bounce.

— Vivian Komori

Quote #49

66 You gain strength, courage, and confidence by every experience in which you really stop to look fear in the face. You are able to say to yourself, 'I lived through this horror. I can take the next thing that comes along.'

— Eleanor Roosevelt

Quote #50

66 I can be changed by what happens to me. But I refuse to be reduced by it.

— Maya Angelou

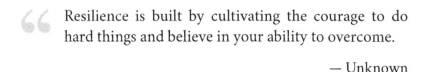

Resilience is built by cultivating the courage to do hard things and believe in your ability to overcome.

— Unknown

QUOTE #52

When everything seems to be going against you, remember that the airplane takes off against the wind, not with it.

— Henry Ford

QUOTE #53

Challenges are what make life interesting and over-coming them is what makes life meaningful.

— Joshua J. Marine

Reflections

1. Think of a recent challenge you faced. How did you respond to it, and what did you learn about yourself in the process?

_____

_____

_____

2. What are some ways you can build resilience in your daily life? Are there any habits or mindsets you can adopt to help you stay strong during tough times?

_____

_____

_____

3. Reflect on a time when you overcame a significant obstacle. How did that experience shape your perspective on future challenges?

_____

_____

_____

Practice

➤ Write down three affirmations that remind you of your strength and resilience. Place them somewhere visible as daily reminders.

➤ Identify a small challenge you are currently facing. Break it down into manageable steps and create a plan to address each step.

➤ Reach out to someone you trust and share a difficult experience you've had. Discuss how you overcame it and what you learned.

Chapter 2

Personal Growth and Self Improvement

As we transition from the themes of overcoming adversity and developing resilience in Chapter 1, we move into the equally vital realm of personal growth and self-improvement in Chapter 2. Building upon the strength and resilience gained from facing life's challenges, this chapter focuses on the ongoing journey of becoming the best version of ourselves. Personal growth is not a destination but a continuous process of learning, evolving, and striving for self-improvement.

Consider the transformative journey of **Maya Angelou**, whose early life was marked by trauma and adversity. Through her resilience and determination, Angelou became a celebrated author, poet, and civil rights activist. Her works, including "I Know Why the Caged Bird Sings," inspire millions to embrace their own narratives of growth and self-improvement. Angelou's quote,

 You may not control all the events that happen to you, but you can decide not to be reduced by them.

encapsulates the essence of personal growth—choosing to rise above circumstances and continually striving for self-betterment.

Another inspiring figure is **Malcolm X**, who transformed his life through education and self-improvement while incarcerated. His dedication to learning and personal development led him to become one of the most influential leaders in the fight for civil rights. Malcolm X's journey from a troubled past to a powerful advocate for change demonstrates the profound impact of personal growth. His words,

 Education is the passport to the future, for tomorrow belongs to those who prepare for it today.

remind us that investing in ourselves through continuous learning is key to unlocking our full potential.

In this chapter, you will find quotes that encourage you to embark on your own journey of personal growth and self-improvement. These insights serve as reminders that no matter where you start, the commitment to bettering yourself can lead to profound transformations. Let these words inspire you to embrace change, seek new knowledge, and strive for continuous self-improvement, building on the resilience you have cultivated to create a life of purpose and fulfillment.

~

Quote #54

Personal development is the belief that you are worth the effort, time, and energy needed to develop yourself.

— Denis Waitley

Quote #55

Be not afraid of growing slowly; be afraid only of standing still.

— Chinese Proverb

Quote #56

Growth is painful. Change is painful. But nothing is as painful as staying stuck somewhere you don't belong.

— Mandy Hale

Quote #57

66 Growth is the only evidence of life.

— John Henry Newman

Quote #58

66 One can choose to go back toward safety or forward toward growth. Growth must be chosen again and again; fear must be overcome again and again.

— Abraham Maslow

Quote #59

66 If it doesn't challenge you, it won't change you.

— Fred DeVito

Quote #60

66 The only person you are destined to become is the person you decide to be.

— Ralph Waldo Emerson

Quote #61

66 What you get by achieving your goals is not as important as what you become by achieving your goals.

— Zig Ziglar

Quote #62

“ We cannot become what we need to be by remaining what we are.

— Max De Pree

Quote #63

“ Be patient with yourself. Self-growth is tender; it's holy ground. There's no greater investment.

— Stephen Covey

Quote #64

“ You must have a level of discontent to feel the urge to want to grow.

— Idowu Koyenikan

Quote #65

“ We find comfort among those who agree with us - growth among those who don't.

— Frank A. Clark

Quote #66

“ Don't limit your challenges, challenge your limits.

— Jerry Dunn

Quote #67

66 Life is growth. If we stop growing, technically and spiritually, we are as good as dead.

— Morihei Ueshiba

Quote #68

66 The only limit to your impact is your imagination and commitment.

— Tony Robbins

Quote #69

66 The beautiful journey of today can only begin when we learn to let go of yesterday.

— Steve Maraboli

Quote #70

66 Don't go through life, grow through life.

— Eric Butterworth

Quote #71

66 There are no great limits to growth because there are no limits of human intelligence, imagination, and wonder.

— Ronald Reagan

Quote #72

❝ Personal growth starts when you start accepting your own weaknesses.

— Jean Vanie

Quote #73

❝ You grow up the day you have your first real laugh at yourself.

— Ethel Barrymore

Quote #74

❝ There is no growth without change, no change without fear or loss and no loss without pain.

— Rick Warren

Quote #75

❝ The mind that opens to a new idea never returns to its original size.

— Albert Einstein

Quote #76

❝ You cannot dream yourself into a character; you must hammer and forge yourself one.

— Henry David Thoreau

QUOTE #77

" The fastest way to change yourself is to hang out with people who are already the way you want to be.

— Reid Hoffman

QUOTE #78

" Change is the end result of all true learning.

— Leo Buscaglia

QUOTE #79

" Man's main task in life is to give birth to himself, to become what he potentially is.

— Erich Fromm

QUOTE #80

" It is not as much about who you used to be, as it is about who you choose to be.

— Sanhita Baruah

QUOTE #81

" We delight in the beauty of the butterfly, but rarely admit the changes it has gone through to achieve that beauty.

— Maya Angelou

Quote #82

❝ Push yourself because no one else is going to do it for you.

— Unknown

Quote #83

❝ Personal growth is not a matter of learning new information but of unlearning old limits.

— Alan Cohen

Quote #84

❝ Success is not to be pursued; it is to be attracted by the person you become.

— Jim Rohn

Quote #85

❝ If you always do what you've always done, you'll always be where you've always been.

— T.D. Jakes

Quote #86

❝ Be the change that you wish to see in the world.

— Mahatma Gandhi

~

Reflections

1. What is one area of your life where you would like to see personal growth? Why is this important to you?

---

2. Think about a time when you felt you had grown as a person. What prompted this growth, and how did it impact you?

---

3. What are some habits or behaviors that you believe are holding you back from reaching your full potential?

Practice

➤ Set a specific, achievable goal for personal growth. Break it down into smaller steps and create a timeline to track your progress.

➤ Identify a book, course, or resource related to an area of self-improvement you're interested in. Dedicate time each week to engage with this material.

➤ Start a daily journal where you reflect on your personal growth journey. Write about your goals, challenges, and progress.

Chapter 3

Education and Learning

Building upon the themes of personal growth and self-improvement in Chapter 2, Chapter 3 explores the transformative power of education and lifelong learning. While personal growth involves the ongoing process of becoming our best selves, education and learning provide the tools and knowledge necessary to fuel that journey. This chapter celebrates the joy of discovery and the endless possibilities that come with a commitment to learning.

Consider the life of **Malala Yousafzai**, who became an international symbol of the fight for girls' education after surviving an assassination attempt by the Taliban. Her unwavering dedication to learning and her advocacy for education rights have inspired millions around the world. Malala's quote,

 One child, one teacher, one book, one pen can change the world.

underscores the profound impact that education can have on individuals and society as a whole.

Another exemplary figure is **Albert Einstein**, whose insatiable curiosity and love for learning led to some of the most significant scientific breakthroughs of the 20th century. Einstein's journey from a young, inquisitive student to a renowned physicist illustrates the power of intellectual curiosity and the importance of questioning the world around us. His quote,

 Education is not the learning of facts, but the training of the mind to think.

highlights the transformative nature of true education, which goes beyond rote memorization to foster critical thinking and creativity.

In this chapter, you will encounter quotes that celebrate the transformative power of education and the endless possibilities that come with a commitment to learning. These insights encourage you to embrace curiosity, seek new knowledge, and never stop learning, no matter where you are in life. Let these  words inspire you to view education as a lifelong journey, one that continually enriches your mind and broadens your horizons, building on the foundation of personal growth and resilience cultivated in the previous chapters.

QUOTE #87

66 Education is the most powerful weapon which you can use to change the world.

— Nelson Mandela

QUOTE #88

66 The mind is not a vessel to be filled, but a fire to be kindled.

— Plutarch

QUOTE #89

66 The purpose of education is to replace an empty mind with an open one.

— Malcolm Forbes

QUOTE #90

66 The only person who is educated is the one who has learned how to learn and change.

— Carl Rogers

QUOTE #91

66 Live as if you were to die tomorrow. Learn as if you were to live forever.

— Mahatma Gandhi

Education is what remains after one has forgotten what one has learned in school.

— Albert Einstein

Quote #93

The whole purpose of education is to turn mirrors into windows.

— Sydney J. Harris

Quote #94

It is the mark of an educated mind to be able to entertain a thought without accepting it.

— Aristotle

Quote #95

The only real mistake is the one from which we learn nothing.

— Henry Ford

Quote #96

Education is the ability to listen to almost anything without losing your temper or your self-confidence.

— Robert Frost

Quote #97

❝ Learning never exhausts the mind.

— Leonardo da Vinci

Quote #98

❝ The only true wisdom is in knowing you know nothing.

— Socrates

Quote #99

❝ It is what we know already that often prevents us from learning.

— Claude Bernard

Quote #100

❝ The function of education is to teach one to think intensively and to think critically. Intelligence plus character – that is the goal of true education.

— Martin Luther King Jr.

Quote #101

❝ What we learn with pleasure we never forget.

— Alfred Mercier

QUOTE #102

" Tell me and I forget, teach me and I may remember, involve me and I learn.

— Benjamin Franklin

QUOTE #103

" Education is the key to unlock the golden door of freedom.

— George Washington Carver

QUOTE #104

" Learning is not attained by chance, it must be sought for with ardor and diligence.

— Abigail Adams

QUOTE #105

" Anyone who stops learning is old, whether at twenty or eighty. Anyone who keeps learning stays young.

— Henry Ford

QUOTE #106

" An investment in knowledge pays the best interest.

— Benjamin Franklin

Quote #107

66 You can teach a student a lesson for a day; but if you can teach him to learn by creating curiosity, he will continue the learning process as long as he lives.

— Clay P. Bedford

Quote #108

66 In learning you will teach, and in teaching you will learn.

— Phil Collins

Quote #109

66 Education is not preparation for life; education is life itself.

— John Dewey

Quote #110

66 The beautiful thing about learning is that no one can take it away from you.

— B.B. King

Quote #111

““ Teaching is not about answering questions but about raising questions – opening doors for them in places that they could not imagine.

— Yawar Baig

Quote #112

““ Develop a passion for learning. If you do, you will never cease to grow.

— Anthony J. D'Angelo

Quote #113

““ Learning is not the product of teaching. Learning is the product of the activity of learners.

— John Holt

Quote #114

““ Education is a progressive discovery of our own ignorance.

— Will Durant

  He who learns but does not think, is lost! He who thinks but does not learn is in great danger.

— Confucius

  I am always ready to learn although I do not always like being taught.

— Winston Churchill

～

Reflections

1. What subjects or topics are you passionate about learning? How can you incorporate more of these into your life?

_____

_____

_____

2. Reflect on a recent learning experience. What did you find most rewarding or challenging about it?

_____

_____

_____

3. How do you typically approach new learning opportunities? Are there ways you can enhance your learning process?

_____

_____

_____

Practice

➤ Commit to learning something new every week. It could be a new skill, a piece of information, or an interesting fact.

➤ Join a group or community related to an area you want to learn more about. Engaging with others can enhance your learning experience.

➤ Set aside a dedicated time each day or week for reading or studying something that interests you. Make this a regular part of your routine.

Chapter 4

Self-Love and Acceptance

Following the exploration of education and learning in Chapter 3, Chapter 4 turns inward to focus on self-love and acceptance. While education empowers us with knowledge and skills, self-love and acceptance provide the emotional foundation necessary for a fulfilling life. This chapter emphasizes the importance of embracing who we are, recognizing our intrinsic worth, and cultivating a compassionate relationship with ourselves.

Consider the journey of **Brené Brown**, a research professor and author whose work on vulnerability and self-compassion has resonated with millions. Brown's insights into the power of embracing our imperfections have helped countless individuals learn to love and accept themselves fully. Her quote,

 Owning our story and loving ourselves through that process is the bravest thing that we will ever do.

highlights the courage it takes to practice self-love and acceptance.

Another powerful example is the life of **Lizzo**, the Grammy-winning artist known for her unapologetic self-love and body positivity. Lizzo's message of embracing one's uniqueness and rejecting societal pressures has inspired a global movement of self-acceptance. Her quote,

> Self-care is in the little moments—bathing, breathing, and eating good food. It's about saying no and having boundaries.

underscores the importance of taking care of oneself and setting healthy boundaries as acts of self-love.

In this chapter, you will find quotes that encourage you to practice self-love and acceptance, reminding you that your worth is inherent and not dependent on external validation. These insights serve as gentle reminders to treat yourself with the same kindness and compassion that you extend to others. Let these words inspire you to embrace your unique qualities, forgive yourself for past mistakes, and cultivate a deep sense of love and acceptance within. By doing so, you will build a strong emotional foundation that enhances every aspect of your life, from personal growth to relationships and beyond.

QUOTE #117

> You yourself, as much as anybody in the entire universe, deserve your love and affection.

— Buddha

QUOTE #118

To love oneself is the beginning of a life-long romance.

— Oscar Wilde

QUOTE #119

Low self-esteem is like driving through life with your hand-brake on.

— Maxwell Maltz

QUOTE #120

Your problem is you're... too busy holding onto your unworthiness.

— Ram Dass

QUOTE #121

Remember, you have been criticizing yourself for years and it hasn't worked. Try approving of yourself and see what happens.

— Louise L. Hay

QUOTE #122

Loving yourself isn't vanity. It's sanity.

— Katrina Mayer

QUOTE #123

66 You're always with yourself, so you might as well enjoy the company.

— Diane Von Furstenberg

QUOTE #124

66 To fall in love with yourself is the first secret to happiness.

— Robert Morley

QUOTE #125

66 Never be bullied into silence. Never allow yourself to be made a victim. Accept no one's definition of your life, but define yourself.

— Harvey Fierstein

QUOTE #126

66 Self-love, my liege, is not so vile a sin, as self-neglecting.

— William Shakespeare, "Henry V"

QUOTE #127

66 Act as if what you do makes a difference. It does.

— William James

Quote #128

66 Why should we worry about what others think of us? Do we have more confidence in their opinions than we do our own?

— Brigham Young

Quote #129

66 Self-esteem is made up primarily of two things: feeling lovable and feeling capable.

— Jack Canfield

Quote #130

66 A man cannot be comfortable without his own approval.

— Mark Twain

Quote #131

66 To be yourself in a world that is constantly trying to make you something else is the greatest accomplishment.

— Ralph Waldo Emerson

QUOTE #132

❝ Trust yourself. You know more than you think you do.

— Benjamin Spock

QUOTE #133

❝ What lies behind us and what lies before us are tiny matters compared to what lies within us.

— Ralph Waldo Emerson

QUOTE #134

❝ You are very powerful, provided you know how powerful you are.

— Yogi Bhajan

QUOTE #135

❝ Once you embrace your value, talents, and strengths, it neutralizes when others think less of you.

— Rob Liano

QUOTE #136

❝ Self-worth comes from one thing - thinking that you are worthy.

— Wayne Dyer

Quote #137

“ People who want the most approval get the least and the people who need approval the least get the most.

— Wayne Dyer

Quote #138

“ It's not who you are that holds you back, it's who you think you're not.

— Denis Waitley

Quote #139

“ Don't waste your energy trying to change opinions ... Do your thing, and don't care if they like it.

— Tina Fey

Quote #140

“ If you don't believe in yourself, why is anyone else going to believe in you?

— Tom Brady

Quote #141

“ You alone are enough. You have nothing to prove to anybody.

— Maya Angelou

Quote #142

66 Our self-respect tracks our choices. Every time we act in harmony with our authentic self and our heart, we earn our respect. It is that simple. Every choice matters.

— Dan Coppersmith

Quote #143

66 The more you praise and celebrate your life, the more there is in life to celebrate.

— Oprah Winfrey

Quote #144

66 Accept yourself, love yourself, and keep moving forward. If you want to fly, you have to give up what weighs you down.

— Roy T. Bennett

Quote #145

66 Beauty begins the moment you decide to be yourself.

— Coco Chanel

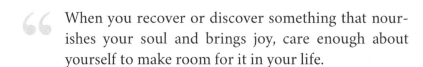 When you recover or discover something that nourishes your soul and brings joy, care enough about yourself to make room for it in your life.

— Jean Shinoda Bolen

QUOTE #147

How you love yourself is how you teach others to love you.

— Rupi Kaur

Reflections

1. What do you appreciate most about yourself? Why is this quality important to you?

_____

_____

_____

2. Think about a time when you felt insecure or critical of yourself. How could you have approached this situation with more self-love and acceptance?

_____

_____

_____

3. How do you currently practice self-care? Are there any additional ways you can show yourself love and kindness?

_____

_____

_____

Practice

➤ Make a list of your strengths and positive qualities. Read it whenever you need a reminder of your worth.

➤ Set aside time each week for a self-care activity that you enjoy, whether it's reading, taking a bath, or going for a walk.

➤ Practice positive self-talk by challenging negative thoughts and replacing them with affirming, compassionate statements.

Chapter 5

Positivity, Gratitude, and Joy

Going beyond the themes of self-love and acceptance in Chapter 4, Chapter 5 invites you to explore the transformative power of positivity, gratitude, and joy. Building on a foundation of self-compassion and acceptance, a positive outlook can enhance every aspect of life, fostering resilience, happiness, and a sense of fulfillment. This chapter celebrates the lighthearted and uplifting moments that make life beautiful, encouraging you to cultivate a mindset of positivity.

Consider the life of **Walt Disney**, who faced numerous setbacks and failures before creating one of the most beloved entertainment empires in the world. Despite early business failures and financial difficulties, Disney's unwavering optimism and imaginative spirit led to the creation of Disneyland and iconic characters that continue to bring joy to millions. His quote,

 All our dreams can come true, if we have the courage to pursue them.

underscores the importance of maintaining a positive outlook and believing in the possibility of dreams.

Another inspiring figure is **Fred Rogers**, the gentle and optimistic host of "Mister Rogers' Neighborhood." Rogers dedicated his life to spreading messages of kindness, acceptance, and joy to children and families through his television program. His ability to find beauty in the simplest moments and his unwavering belief in the goodness of people are reflected in his quote,

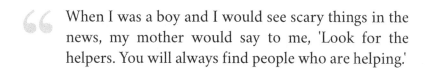 When I was a boy and I would see scary things in the news, my mother would say to me, 'Look for the helpers. You will always find people who are helping.'

This advice encourages us to focus on the positive and the helpers in any situation, fostering a sense of hope and optimism.

In this chapter, you will find quotes that inspire positivity, gratitude, and joy, serving as daily reminders to look for the good in every situation and embrace life with an open heart. These insights encourage you to focus on the bright side, cultivate gratitude, and find joy in the small moments. Let these words uplift your spirit, helping you to foster a positive mindset that enhances your well-being and spreads happiness to those around you. By embracing positivity, gratitude, and joy, you can create a more fulfilling and vibrant life, building on the foundations of self-love, acceptance, and personal growth explored in the previous chapters.

Quote #148

The pessimist sees difficulty in every opportunity. The optimist sees opportunity in every difficulty.

— Winston Churchill

Quote #149

Believe that life is worth living and your belief will help create the fact.

— William James

Quote #150

Optimism is the faith that leads to achievement. Nothing can be done without hope and confidence.

— Helen Keller

Quote #151

" Once you replace negative thoughts with positive ones, you'll start having positive results.

— Willie Nelson

Quote #152

" Gratitude is a divine emotion: it fills the heart, but not to bursting; it warms it, but not to fever.

— Charlotte Brontë

Quote #153

" Things turn out best for the people who make the best of the way things turn out.

— John Wooden

Quote #154

" Let us be grateful to people who make us happy; they are the charming gardeners who make our souls blossom.

— Marcel Proust

Quote #155

❝ Gratitude is a currency that we can mint for ourselves, and spend without fear of bankruptcy.

— Fred De Witt Van Amburgh

Quote #156

❝ In order to carry a positive action we must develop here a positive vision.

— Dalai Lama

Quote #157

❝ The greatest discovery of all time is that a person can change his future by merely changing his attitude.

— Oprah Winfrey

Quote #158

❝ Gratitude unlocks the fullness of life. It turns what we have into enough, and more.

— Melody Beattie

Quote #159

❝ A positive atmosphere nurtures a positive attitude, which is required to take positive action.

— Richard M. DeVos

QUOTE #160

" You must expect great things of yourself before you can do them.

— Michael Jordan

QUOTE #161

" Be thankful for what you have; you'll end up having more. If you concentrate on what you don't have, you will never, ever have enough.

— Oprah Winfrey

QUOTE #162

" If you are positive, you'll see opportunities instead of obstacles.

— Widad Akrawi

QUOTE #163

" Virtually nothing is impossible in this world if you just put your mind to it and maintain a positive attitude.

— Lou Holtz

Quote #164

66 Every day may not be good... but there's something good in every day.

— Alice Morse Earle

Quote #165

66 Success is a state of mind. If you want success, start thinking of yourself as a success.

— Joyce Brothers

Quote #166

66 Dwell on the beauty of life. Watch the stars, and see yourself running with them.

— Marcus Aurelius

Quote #167

66 I am determined to be cheerful and happy in whatever situation I may find myself. For I have learned that the greater part of our misery or unhappiness is determined not by our circumstance but by our disposition.

— Martha Washington

Quote #168

" Perpetual optimism is a force multiplier.

— Colin Powell

Quote #169

" It's a funny thing about life; if you refuse to accept anything but the best, you very often get it.

— W. Somerset Maugham

Quote #170

" The only limit to our realization of tomorrow will be our doubts of today.

— Franklin D. Roosevelt

Quote #171

" Gratitude is the ability to experience life as a gift. It liberates us from the prison of self-preoccupation.

— John Ortberg

Quote #172

" A positive attitude causes a chain reaction of positive thoughts, events, and outcomes. It is a catalyst and it sparks extraordinary results.

— Wade Boggs

QUOTE #173

66 Believe you can and you're halfway there.

— Theodore Roosevelt

QUOTE #174

66 Gratitude is a powerful catalyst for happiness. It's the spark that lights a fire of joy in your soul.

— Amy Collette

QUOTE #175

66 Do not anticipate trouble, or worry about what may never happen. Keep in the sunlight.

— Benjamin Franklin

QUOTE #176

66 Optimism is a happiness magnet. If you stay positive, good things and good people will be drawn to you.

— Mary Lou Retton

QUOTE #177

66 Gratitude makes sense of our past, brings peace for today, and creates a vision for tomorrow.

— Melody Beattie

Quote #178

   A strong, positive self-image is the best possible preparation for success.

— Joyce Brothers

Quote #179

   Appreciation can make a day, even change a life. Your willingness to put it into words is all that is necessary.

— Margaret Cousins

Quote #180

   It is not joy that makes us grateful; it is gratitude that makes us joyful.

— David Steindl-Rast

Quote #181

   Gratitude is the healthiest of all human emotions. The more you express gratitude for what you have, the more likely you will have even more to express gratitude for.

— Zig Ziglar

Quote #182

" No duty is more urgent than giving thanks.

— James Allen

Quote #183

" Gratitude can transform common days into thanks-givings, turn routine jobs into joy, and change ordinary opportunities into blessings.

— William Arthur Ward

Quote #184

" Feeling gratitude and not expressing it is like wrapping a present and not giving it.

— William Arthur Ward

Quote #185

" Gratitude bestows reverence, allowing us to encounter everyday epiphanies, those transcendent moments of awe that change forever how we experience life and the world.

— John Milton

Quote #186

66 Gratitude turns a meal into a feast, a house into a home, a stranger into a friend.

— Melody Beattie

Quote #187

66 When we focus on our gratitude, the tide of disappointment goes out and the tide of love rushes in.

— Kristin Armstrong

Quote #188

66 Gratitude is the inward feeling of kindness received. Thankfulness is the natural impulse to express that feeling. Thanksgiving is the following of that impulse.

— Henry Van Dyke

∾

Reflections

1. What are three things in your life that bring you joy? How can you make more time for these activities or experiences?

_____

_____

_____

2. Reflect on a challenging situation where you maintained a positive outlook. How did this perspective help you navigate the situation?

_____

_____

_____

3. How do you currently express gratitude in your daily life? Are there ways you can incorporate more gratitude practices?

_____

_____

_____

Practice

➤ Start a gratitude journal and write down three things you're grateful for each day.

➤ Identify a positive mantra or affirmation that resonates with you. Repeat it to yourself each morning to set a positive tone for the day.

➤ Take a few minutes each day to smile and laugh, whether through watching a funny video, reading a joke, or recalling a happy memory.

Chapter 6

Creativity and Innovation

Building on the themes of positivity, gratitude, and joy in Chapter 5, Chapter 6 delves into the dynamic realms of creativity and innovation. When we embrace a positive mindset, it fuels our creative potential and opens the door to innovative thinking. This chapter celebrates the power of imagination and the courage to bring new ideas to life, highlighting how creativity and innovation can transform both our personal lives and the world around us.

Consider the legacy of **Steve Jobs**, co-founder of Apple Inc., whose visionary thinking and innovative spirit revolutionized the technology industry. Jobs's relentless pursuit of excellence and his belief in the power of creativity led to groundbreaking products that changed the way we interact with technology. His quote,

 Innovation distinguishes between a leader and a follower.

emphasizes the importance of daring to think differently and the impact of creative leadership.

Another inspiring figure is **Frida Kahlo**, the iconic Mexican artist known for her unique and evocative paintings. Despite enduring significant physical pain and personal challenges, Kahlo's creativity flourished, making her one of the most celebrated artists of the 20th century. Her quote,

 I paint my own reality. The only thing I know is that I paint because I need to, and I paint whatever passes through my head without any other consideration.

underscores the importance of authentic self-expression and the transformative power of creativity.

 In this chapter, you will find quotes that inspire you to unleash your creative potential and embrace innovative thinking. These insights encourage you to think outside the box, take risks, and bring your unique ideas to fruition. Let these words motivate you to explore new possibilities, nurture your imagination, and approach challenges with a creative mindset. By fostering creativity and innovation, you can bring fresh perspectives and solutions to the world, building on the positivity and joy cultivated in the previous chapters. Embrace the transformative power of creativity and let it guide you toward new horizons of discovery and achievement.

Quote #189

❝ Creativity is seeing what everyone else has seen, and thinking what no one else has thought.

— Albert Einstein

Quote #190

❝ You can't use up creativity. The more you use, the more you have.

— Maya Angelou

Quote #191

❝ Creativity involves breaking out of expected patterns in order to look at things in a different way.

— Edward de Bono

Quote #192

❝ Do not be afraid to give up the good to go for the great.

— John D. Rockefeller

Quote #193

66 Imagination is the beginning of creation. You imagine what you desire, you will what you imagine, and at last, you create what you will.

— George Bernard Shaw

Quote #194

66 Creativity is a wild mind and a disciplined eye.

— Dorothy Parker

Quote #195

66 The biggest risk is not taking any risk. In a world that is changing really quickly, the only strategy that is guaranteed to fail is not taking risks.

— Mark Zuckerberg

Quote #196

66 What is now proved was once only imagined.

— William Blake

Quote #197

66 Daring ideas are like chessmen moved forward; they may be beaten, but they may start a winning game.

— Johann Wolfgang von Goethe

Quote #198

66 The true sign of intelligence is not knowledge but imagination.

— Albert Einstein

Quote #199

66 Imagination is more important than knowledge. For knowledge is limited, whereas imagination embraces the entire world.

— Albert Einstein

Quote #200

66 Every act of creation is first an act of destruction.

— Pablo Picasso

Quote #201

66 The world always seems brighter when you've just made something that wasn't there before.

— Neil Gaiman

Quote #202

66 To live a creative life, we must lose our fear of being wrong.

— Joseph Chilton Pearce

To be creative means to be in love with life. You can be creative only if you love life enough that you want to enhance its beauty.

— Osho

QUOTE #204

There is no innovation and creativity without failure. Period.

— Brené Brown

QUOTE #205

Creativity requires the courage to let go of certainties.

— Erich Fromm

QUOTE #206

The only way to discover the limits of the possible is to go beyond them into the impossible.

— Arthur C. Clarke

QUOTE #207

The best way to predict the future is to invent it.

— Alan Kay

" Innovation is taking two things that already exist and putting them together in a new way.

— Tom Freston

QUOTE #209

" Creativity is allowing yourself to make mistakes. Art is knowing which ones to keep.

— Scott Adams

QUOTE #210

" The chief enemy of creativity is 'good' sense.

— Pablo Picasso

QUOTE #211

" If you're not failing every now and again, it's a sign you're not doing anything very innovative.

— Woody Allen

QUOTE #212

" Creativity is piercing the mundane to find the marvelous.

— Bill Moyers

Quote #213

66 Without deviation from the norm, progress is not possible.

— Frank Zappa

Quote #214

66 Innovation is the ability to see change as an opportunity - not a threat.

— Steve Jobs

Quote #215

66 Genius means little more than the faculty of perceiving in an unhabitual way.

— William James

Quote #216

66 To invent, you need a good imagination and a pile of junk.

— Thomas Edison

Quote #217

66 Creativity is the power to connect the seemingly unconnected.

— William Plomer

~

Reflections

1. When do you feel most creative? What activities or environments inspire your creativity?

_____

_____

_____

2. Think about a time when you solved a problem creatively. What approach did you take, and what was the outcome?

_____

_____

_____

3. How do you currently nurture your creative side? Are there new ways you can explore or express your creativity?

_____

_____

_____

Practice

➤ Set aside time each week for a creative activity, whether it's drawing, writing, cooking, or another hobby you enjoy.

➤ Challenge yourself to think outside the box by brainstorming new solutions to a current problem or project.

➤ Create a vision board with images and words that inspire you. Use it as a visual reminder of your creative goals and aspirations.

Chapter 7

Goal Setting, Achievement, and Success

Extending beyond the concepts of creativity and innovation from Chapter 6, Chapter 7 gets into the practical applications of these traits: goal setting, achievement, and success. While creativity ignites the spark of new ideas, it is through clear goals and determined action that these ideas are transformed into tangible successes. This chapter celebrates the power of vision and perseverance, offering insights into how setting and achieving goals can lead to profound personal and professional fulfillment.

One remarkable example of this journey is the story of **Thomas Edison**, whose inventive spirit revolutionized the modern world. Despite facing numerous failures and setbacks, Edison's unwavering commitment to his goals led to the invention of the electric light bulb and many other groundbreaking technologies. His famous words,

 I have not failed. I've just found 10,000 ways that won't work.

epitomize the resilience and determination required to achieve greatness.

Similarly, the life of **Oprah Winfrey** illustrates how clear goal setting and relentless pursuit can overcome even the most challenging circumstances. Rising from poverty and adversity, Winfrey set her sights on a career in media, and through hard work and dedication, she became one of the most influential and successful figures in television and beyond. Her journey underscores the importance of having a clear vision and the perseverance to see it through, no matter the obstacles.

In this chapter, the quotes you will encounter are more than just words; they are blueprints for success, encouraging you to define your aspirations and pursue them with unwavering determination. By setting clear goals and committing to their achievement, you can transform your dreams into reality, much like the luminaries who have walked this path before you. Let these insights inspire you to take the next step towards your own success, fueled by the creativity and resilience cultivated in the previous chapters.

QUOTE #218

Opportunity is missed by most people because it is dressed in overalls and looks like work.

— Thomas Edison

Setting goals is the first step in turning the invisible into the visible.

— Tony Robbins

Success is not the key to happiness. Happiness is the key to success. If you love what you are doing, you will be successful.

— Albert Schweitzer

Goals are the fuel in the furnace of achievement.

— Brian Tracy

What you get by achieving your goals is not as important as what you become by achieving your goals.

— Zig Ziglar

If you aim at nothing, you will hit it every time.

— Zig Ziglar

Quote #224

66 To reach a port, we must sail—Sail, not tie at anchor
—Sail, not drift.

— Franklin D. Roosevelt

Quote #225

66 By recording your dreams and goals on paper, you
set in motion the process of becoming the person
you most want to be. Put your future in good hands
— your own.

— Mark Victor Hansen

Quote #226

66 Success is not how high you have climbed, but how
you make a positive difference to the world.

— Roy T. Bennett

Quote #227

66 People with goals succeed because they know where
they're going.

— Earl Nightingale

Quote #228

  The only way to achieve the impossible is to believe it is possible.

— Charles Kingsleigh

Quote #229

  If you want to be happy, set a goal that commands your thoughts, liberates your energy, and inspires your hopes.

— Andrew Carnegie

Quote #230

  Success is the progressive realization of a worthy goal or ideal.

— Earl Nightingale

Quote #231

  The only thing standing between you and your goal is the bogus story you keep telling yourself as to why you can't achieve it.

— Jordan Belfort

Quote #232

" You are never too old to set another goal or to dream a new dream.

— C.S. Lewis

Quote #233

" Your goals are the road maps that guide you and show you what is possible for your life.

— Les Brown

Quote #234

" Obstacles are those frightful things you see when you take your eyes off your goal.

— Henry Ford

Quote #235

" Our goals can only be reached through a vehicle of a plan, in which we must fervently believe, and upon which we must vigorously act. There is no other route to success.

— Pablo Picasso

QUOTE #236

Don't watch the clock; do what it does. Keep going.

— Sam Levenson

QUOTE #237

Success is the result of hard work, busting your butt every day for years on end without cutting corners or taking shortcuts.

— Ronda Rousey

QUOTE #238

The journey of a thousand miles begins with one step.

— Lao Tzu

QUOTE #239

A dream becomes a goal when action is taken toward its achievement.

— Bo Bennett

QUOTE #240

Vision without action is daydream. Action without vision is nightmare.

— Japanese Proverb

Success is stumbling from failure to failure with no loss of enthusiasm.

— Winston Churchill

I find that the harder I work, the more luck I seem to have.

— Thomas Jefferson

Go as far as you can see; when you get there, you'll be able to see further.

— Thomas Carlyle

I am not a product of my circumstances. I am a product of my decisions.

— Stephen Covey

The man who moves a mountain begins by carrying away small stones.

— Confucius

Quote #246

Do not wait to strike till the iron is hot, but make it hot by striking.

— William Butler Yeats

Quote #247

I've missed more than 9000 shots in my career. I've lost almost 300 games. 26 times I've been trusted to take the game-winning shot and missed. I've failed over and over and over again in my life. And that is why I succeed.

— Michael Jordan

Quote #248

Nothing will work unless you do.

— Maya Angelou

Quote #249

A professional is someone who can do his best work when he doesn't feel like it.

— Alistair Cooke

QUOTE #250

You miss 100% of the shots you don't take.

— Wayne Gretzky

QUOTE #251

Don't judge each day by the harvest you reap but by the seeds that you plant.

— Robert Louis Stevenson

QUOTE #252

Start where you are. Use what you have. Do what you can.

— Arthur Ashe

QUOTE #253

It's not the days in your life, but the life in your days that counts.

— Brian White

~

Reflections

1. What is one long-term goal you have? Why is this goal important to you, and how will it impact your life?

_____

_____

_____

2. Reflect on a past achievement. What steps did you take to reach this goal, and what did you learn from the experience?

_____

_____

_____

3. How do you handle setbacks when working towards a goal? What strategies can you use to stay motivated and focused?

_____

_____

_____

Practice

➤ Write down your top three goals for the next year. Break each goal into smaller, actionable steps and create a timeline for achieving them.

➤ Identify a role model who has achieved similar goals. Study their journey and note any strategies or lessons you can apply to your own goals.

➤ Celebrate your progress, no matter how small. Take time to acknowledge and reward yourself for the steps you've taken towards your goals.

Chapter 8

Empathy and Kindness

Following the pursuit of goals and success in Chapter 7, Chapter 8 turns our focus towards the equally vital human qualities of empathy and kindness. While ambition and achievement drive personal and professional growth, empathy and kindness are the glue that binds communities together, fostering deeper connections and a more compassionate world. This chapter underscores the importance of understanding and caring for others, which enriches our lives and the lives of those around us.

Consider the life of **Mahatma Gandhi**, whose profound empathy and unwavering commitment to nonviolence led to the liberation of India. Gandhi's belief in the power of kindness and understanding transcended political strategy; it was a philosophy of life. His famous quote,

 The best way to find yourself is to lose yourself in the service of others.

encapsulates the transformative power of empathy and the lasting impact of living a life grounded in compassion.

Another inspiring example is **Mother Teresa**, who dedicated her life to serving the poorest of the poor. Her acts of kindness and selfless service have left an indelible mark on the world, reminding us that empathy in action can change lives. She once said,

 Not all of us can do great things. But we can do small things with great love.

This powerful message highlights that every act of kindness, no matter how small, contributes to the greater good.

In this chapter, you will find quotes that encourage you to cultivate empathy and practice kindness in your daily life. These principles are not only foundational for building strong, supportive relationships but also essential for creating a more inclusive and understanding world. Reflect on these quotes as you navigate your journey, remembering that true success is measured not just by personal achievements but by the positive impact we have on others. Let empathy and kindness guide your actions, enhancing both your life and the lives of those you touch.

QUOTE #254

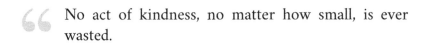 No act of kindness, no matter how small, is ever wasted.

— Aesop

QUOTE #255

Whenever you feel like criticizing any one... just remember that all the people in this world haven't had the advantages that you've had.

— F. Scott Fitzgerald

QUOTE #256

Empathy is about finding echoes of another person in yourself.

— Mohsin Hamid

Quote #257

❝ You never really understand a person until you consider things from his point of view... Until you climb inside of his skin and walk around in it.

— Harper Lee, *To Kill a Mockingbird*

Quote #258

❝ Be kind, for everyone you meet is fighting a harder battle.

— Plato

Quote #259

❝ The only way to tell the truth is to speak with kindness. Only the words of a loving man can be heard.

— Henry David Thoreau

Quote #260

❝ Kindness begins with the understanding that we all struggle.

— Charles Glassman

Quote #261

❝ I've learned that people will forget what you said, people will forget what you did, but people will never forget how you made them feel.

— Maya Angelou

Quote #262

❝ Kindness is a language which the deaf can hear and the blind can see.

— Mark Twain

Quote #263

❝ Tenderness and kindness are not signs of weakness and despair, but manifestations of strength and resolution.

— Kahlil Gibran

Quote #264

❝ A kind gesture can reach a wound that only compassion can heal.

— Steve Maraboli

Quote #265

" Kindness can transform someone's dark moment with a blaze of light. You'll never know how much your caring matters.

— Amy Leigh Mercree

Quote #266

" Compassion and tolerance are not a sign of weakness, but a sign of strength.

— Dalai Lama

Quote #267

" We think too much and feel too little. More than machinery, we need humanity; more than cleverness, we need kindness and gentleness.

— Charlie Chaplin

Quote #268

" When you are kind to others, it not only changes you, it changes the world.

— Harold Kushner

QUOTE #269

66 Empathy is the starting point for creating a community and taking action. It's the impetus for creating change.

— Max Carver

QUOTE #270

66 Kind words can be short and easy to speak, but their echoes are truly endless.

— Mother Teresa

QUOTE #271

66 True empathy requires that you step outside your own emotions to view things entirely from the perspective of the other person.

— Unknown

QUOTE #272

66 Kindness is more important than wisdom, and the recognition of this is the beginning of wisdom.

— Theodore Isaac Rubin

Quote #273

66 If we have no peace, it is because we have forgotten that we belong to each other.

— Mother Teresa

Quote #274

66 Remember there's no such thing as a small act of kindness. Every act creates a ripple with no logical end.

— Scott Adams

Quote #275

66 Empathy is the lovefire of sweet remembrance and shared understanding.

— John Eaton

Quote #276

66 Human kindness has never weakened the stamina or softened the fiber of a free people. A nation does not have to be cruel to be tough.

— Franklin D. Roosevelt

Quote #277

❝ Kindness is the mark we leave on the world.

— Raktivist

Quote #278

❝ Carry out a random act of kindness, with no expectation of reward, safe in the knowledge that one day someone might do the same for you.

— Princess Diana

Quote #279

❝ The simplest acts of kindness are by far more powerful than a thousand heads bowing in prayer.

— Mahatma Gandhi

Quote #280

❝ A single act of kindness throws out roots in all directions, and the roots spring up and make new trees.

— Amelia Earhart

Quote #281

❝ If you want others to be happy, practice compassion. If you want to be happy, practice compassion.

— Dalai Lama

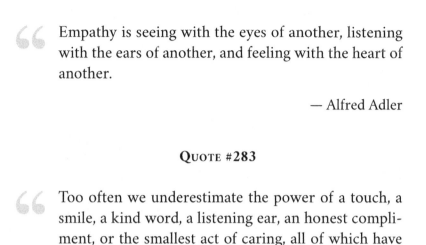

Quote #282

Empathy is seeing with the eyes of another, listening with the ears of another, and feeling with the heart of another.

— Alfred Adler

Quote #283

Too often we underestimate the power of a touch, a smile, a kind word, a listening ear, an honest compliment, or the smallest act of caring, all of which have the potential to turn a life around.

— Leo Buscaglia

~

Reflections

1. Think of a recent interaction where you showed empathy or kindness. How did it affect the other person and yourself?

_____

_____

_____

Empathy and Kindness 93

2. Reflect on a time when someone showed you empathy or kindness. How did it impact your relationship with that person?

_____

_____

_____

3. How do you currently practice empathy and kindness in your daily life? Are there ways you can enhance these practices?

_____

_____

_____

Practice

➤ Perform a random act of kindness each day, whether it's complimenting someone, helping a stranger, or sending a kind message.

➤ Practice active listening in your conversations. Focus on understanding the other person's perspective without interrupting or judging.

➤ Volunteer for a cause or organization you care about. Giving your time and energy to help others can strengthen your sense of empathy and community.

Chapter 9

Relationships and Community

Building on the principles of empathy and kindness explored in Chapter 8, Chapter 9 delves into the vital importance of relationships and community. While empathy and kindness form the foundation of our interactions, it is through nurturing relationships and fostering a sense of community that we create a supportive network, enriching our lives and the lives of those around us. This chapter celebrates the power of human connection and the strength we find in unity.

Consider the life of **Martin Luther King Jr.**, whose dedication to civil rights and equality was deeply rooted in his belief in the power of community and solidarity. King's leadership during the Civil Rights Movement emphasized the importance of coming together to fight for justice and human dignity. His quote,

 Life's most persistent and urgent question is, 'What are you doing for others?'

underscores the significance of building strong relationships and contributing to the well-being of our communities.

Another inspiring figure is **Eleanor Roosevelt**, who, as First Lady of the United States and a tireless human rights advocate, worked to foster a sense of global community and mutual understanding. Her efforts in drafting the Universal Declaration of Human Rights reflect her deep commitment to creating a world where everyone is valued and respected. Roosevelt's quote,

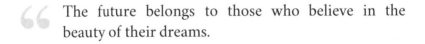 The future belongs to those who believe in the beauty of their dreams.

encourages us to believe in our collective dreams and work together to create a better world.

In this chapter, the quotes you will encounter remind you of the importance of cultivating meaningful relationships and contributing to your community. They emphasize that true fulfillment comes not just from individual success but from the bonds we build and the positive influence we have on those around us. Let these insights inspire you to strengthen your connections and actively participate in creating a vibrant, supportive community. Through collaboration and mutual support, we can achieve far more together than we ever could alone.

Quote #284

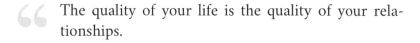
The quality of your life is the quality of your relationships.

— Tony Robbins

Quote #285

In the sweetness of friendship let there be laughter, and sharing of pleasures.

— Kahlil Gibran

Quote #286

A true community is not just about being geographically close to someone or part of the same social web network. It's about feeling connected and responsible for what happens.

— Yehuda Berg

Quote #287

❝ The best thing to hold onto in life is each other.

— Audrey Hepburn

Quote #288

❝ Connection is why we're here; it is what gives purpose and meaning to our lives.

— Brené Brown

Quote #289

❝ The most important thing in the world is family and love.

— John Wooden

Quote #290

❝ The bond that links your true family is not one of blood, but of respect and joy in each other's life.

— Richard Bach

Quote #291

❝ A real friend is one who walks in when the rest of the world walks out.

— Walter Winchell

Quote #292

66 Love and compassion are necessities, not luxuries. Without them, humanity cannot survive.

— Dalai Lama

Quote #293

66 To love and be loved is to feel the sun from both sides.

— David Viscott

Quote #294

66 The love of family and the admiration of friends is much more important than wealth and privilege.

— Charles Kuralt

Quote #295

66 A single rose can be my garden... a single friend, my world.

— Leo Buscaglia

Quote #296

66 One of the most beautiful qualities of true friendship is to understand and to be understood.

— Seneca

Quote #297

" A friend is someone who knows all about you and still loves you.

— Elbert Hubbard

Quote #298

" Community is much more than belonging to something; it's about doing something together that makes belonging matter.

— Brian Solis

Quote #299

" The only way to have a friend is to be one.

— Ralph Waldo Emerson

Quote #300

" No man is an island, entire of itself; every man is a piece of the continent, a part of the main.

— John Donne

Quote #301

" In every conceivable manner, the family is a link to our past, bridge to our future.

— Alex Haley

Quote #302

“ True friends are those rare people who come to find you in dark places and lead you back to the light.

— Unknown

Quote #303

“ If you want to go fast, go alone. If you want to go far, go together.

— African Proverb

Quote #304

“ There is no exercise better for the heart than reaching down and lifting people up.

— John Holmes

Quote #305

“ To the world you may be one person, but to one person you may be the world.

— Dr. Seuss

Quote #306

“ Happiness is only real when shared.

— Jon Krakauer

Quote #307

66 We were born to unite with our fellow men, and to join in community with the human race.

— Cicero

Quote #308

66 The love in your heart wasn't put there to stay. Love isn't love until you give it away.

— Oscar Hammerstein II

Quote #309

66 We make a living by what we get, but we make a life by what we give.

— Winston Churchill

Quote #310

66 True community is based upon equality, mutuality, and reciprocity. It affirms the richness of individual diversity as well as the common human ties that bind us together.

— Pauli Murray

Reflections

1. What qualities do you value most in your relationships? How can you cultivate these qualities in your interactions with others?

_____

_____

_____

2. Think about a strong relationship you have. What makes this relationship successful, and what can you learn from it to apply to other relationships?

_____

_____

_____

3. How do you contribute to your community? Are there new ways you can get involved or support those around you?

_____

_____

_____

Practice

➤ Reach out to a friend or family member you haven't spoken to in a while. Reconnect and express your appreciation for them.

➤ Organize or participate in a community event, such as a neighborhood clean-up, charity drive, or social gathering.

➤ Practice gratitude in your relationships by regularly expressing appreciation and thanks to those around you.

Chapter 10

Teamwork and Collaboration

Following the exploration of relationships and community in Chapter 9, Chapter 10 highlights the power of teamwork and collaboration. While strong relationships and a sense of community provide the foundation, it is through effective teamwork and collaboration that we achieve collective goals and drive progress. This chapter celebrates the synergy that arises when individuals come together to work towards a common purpose, highlighting how unity and cooperation can lead to extraordinary outcomes.

A shining example of the power of teamwork is the story of the Apollo 11 mission, which successfully landed humans on the moon in 1969. This monumental achievement was the result of the collaborative efforts of thousands of scientists, engineers, and astronauts, all working towards a single goal. **Neil Armstrong**'s famous words,

 That's one small step for man, one giant leap for mankind.

underscore the collective triumph of teamwork and the incredible feats that can be accomplished when we join forces.

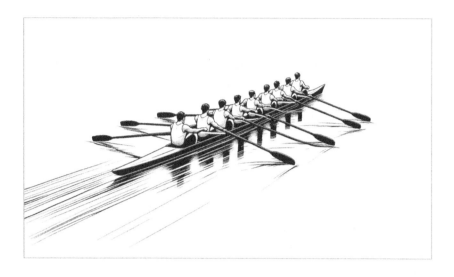

Another inspiring figure is **Michael Jordan**, whose basketball career is a testament to the power of teamwork. While Jordan's individual talent was undeniable, it was his ability to work seamlessly with his teammates that led the Chicago Bulls to six NBA championships. His quote,

 Talent wins games, but teamwork and intelligence win championships.

highlights the importance of collaboration in achieving sustained success.

In this chapter, the quotes you will discover emphasize the importance of working together and the remarkable results that can be achieved through collaboration. They illustrate that while individual effort is important, it is the collective power of a united team that drives true progress. Let these insights inspire you to embrace teamwork in your personal and professional life, recognizing that together, we can accomplish far more than we ever could alone. By fostering a spirit of collaboration and mutual support, we can create a world where everyone thrives.

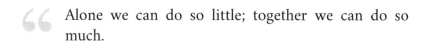

QUOTE #311

66 Alone we can do so little; together we can do so much.

— Helen Keller

QUOTE #312

66 Coming together is a beginning. Keeping together is progress. Working together is success.

— Henry Ford

QUOTE #313

66 Teamwork is the secret that makes common people achieve uncommon results.

— Ifeanyi Enoch Onuoha

QUOTE #314

66 None of us is as smart as all of us.

— Ken Blanchard

Quote #315

66 The best teamwork comes from men who are working independently toward one goal in unison.

— James Cash Penney

Quote #316

66 It is literally true that you can succeed best and quickest by helping others to succeed.

— Napolean Hill

Quote #317

66 Teamwork divides the task and multiplies the success.

— Unknown

Quote #318

66 Find a group of people who challenge and inspire you, spend a lot of time with them, and it will change your life.

— Amy Poehler

Quote #319

66 Teamwork makes the dream work.

— John C. Maxwell

Quote #320

" Individually, we are one drop. Together, we are an ocean.

— Ryunosuke Satoro

Quote #321

" The way a team plays as a whole determines its success. You may have the greatest bunch of individual stars in the world, but if they don't play together, the club won't be worth a dime.

— Babe Ruth

Quote #322

" No one can whistle a symphony. It takes a whole orchestra to play it.

— H.E. Luccock

Quote #323

" Great things in business are never done by one person; they're done by a team of people.

— Steve Jobs

Quote #324

A single leaf working alone provides no shade.

— Chuck Page

Quote #325

Unity is strength... when there is teamwork and collaboration, wonderful things can be achieved.

— Mattie Stepanek

Quote #326

If you want to lift yourself up, lift up someone else.

— Booker T. Washington

Quote #327

Teamwork is the ability to work together toward a common vision. The ability to direct individual accomplishments toward organizational objectives. It is the fuel that allows common people to attain uncommon results.

— Andrew Carnegie

Quote #328

No individual can win a game by himself.

— Pelé

Quote #329

66 Many ideas grow better when transplanted into another mind than the one where they sprang up.

— Oliver Wendell Holmes

Quote #330

66 When you hand good people possibility, they do great things.

— Biz Stone

Quote #331

66 Collaboration allows us to know more than we are capable of knowing by ourselves.

— Paul Solarz

Quote #332

66 The main ingredient of stardom is the rest of the team.

— John Wooden

Quote #333

66 It is amazing what you can accomplish if you do not care who gets the credit.

— Harry S. Truman

You don't get harmony when everybody sings the same note.

— Doug Floyd

QUOTE #335

The way to achieve your own success is to be willing to help somebody else get it first.

— Iyanla Vanzant

QUOTE #336

When 'I' is replaced by 'We,' even illness becomes wellness.

— Malcolm X

~

Reflections

1. Think about a time when you worked on a successful team. What factors contributed to the team's success, and what role did you play?

_____

_____

_____

2. Reflect on a challenging team experience. What did you learn from this situation, and how can you apply these lessons to future collaborations?

_____

_____

_____

3. How do you typically contribute to a team? Are there ways you can enhance your teamwork skills?

_____

_____

_____

Practice

➤ Identify a current project or goal that could benefit from collaboration. Reach out to others for their input and ideas.

➤ Practice clear and open communication with your team members. Ensure everyone is on the same page and feels heard and valued.

➤ Set up regular check-ins with your team to discuss progress, address any challenges, and celebrate successes together.

Chapter 11

Mindfulness and Inner Peace

After exploring the themes of teamwork and collaboration in Chapter 10, Chapter 11 shifts focus inward to mindfulness and inner peace. While working together and achieving collective goals are crucial, it is equally important to cultivate a sense of tranquility and awareness within ourselves. This chapter celebrates the practice of mindfulness as a pathway to inner peace, offering insights into how a calm and centered mind can enhance every aspect of our lives.

One of the most profound examples of mindfulness is **Thích Nhất Hạnh**, a Vietnamese Buddhist monk whose teachings on peace and mindfulness have touched millions around the world. His life's work, centered on the practice of being fully present, emphasizes the importance of inner peace as a foundation for external harmony. His quote,

 The present moment is filled with joy and happiness. If you are attentive, you will see it.

reminds us of the simple yet profound power of living in the now.

Another inspiring figure is **Eckhart Tolle**, whose book "The Power of Now" has become a cornerstone for those seeking spiritual awakening and mindfulness. Tolle's teachings focus on the importance of relinquishing past regrets and future anxieties to embrace the present moment fully. His quote,

 Realize deeply that the present moment is all you ever have. Make the Now the primary focus of your life.

encapsulates the essence of his message and the transformative potential of mindfulness.

In this chapter, the quotes you will find guide you toward a deeper understanding of mindfulness and the peace it brings. They encourage you to cultivate a practice of being present, to find calm amidst the chaos, and to connect with your inner self. By integrating mindfulness into your daily routine, you can enhance your well-being, improve your relationships, and navigate life's challenges with greater ease and clarity. Let these insights inspire you to embrace a mindful approach to life, fostering inner peace that radiates outward, enriching your journey and those of everyone you encounter.

Quote #337

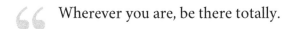 Wherever you are, be there totally.

— Eckhart Tolle

Quote #338

Mindfulness helps you go home to the present. And every time you go there and recognize a condition of happiness that you have, happiness comes.

— Thích Nhất Hạnh

Quote #339

The present moment is the only time over which we have dominion.

— Thích Nhất Hạnh

“ In today's rush, we all think too much — seek too much — want too much — and forget about the joy of just being.

— Eckhart Tolle

QUOTE #341

“ The only way to live is by accepting each minute as an unrepeatable miracle.

— Tara Brach

QUOTE #342

“ Waking up this morning, I smile. Twenty-four brand new hours are before me. I vow to live fully in each moment.

— Thích Nhất Hạnh

QUOTE #343

“ Be happy in the moment, that's enough. Each moment is all we need, not more.

— Mother Teresa

Quote #344

“ Do not dwell in the past, do not dream of the future, concentrate the mind on the present moment.

— Buddha

Quote #345

“ Let go of your mind and then be mindful. Close your ears and listen!

— Rumi

Quote #346

“ Mindfulness is the aware, balanced acceptance of the present experience. It isn't more complicated than that.

— Sylvia Boorstein

Quote #347

“ If you want to conquer the anxiety of life, live in the moment, live in the breath.

— Amit Ray

Quote #348

66 The best way to capture moments is to pay attention. This is how we cultivate mindfulness.

— Jon Kabat-Zinn

Quote #349

66 Looking at beauty in the world is the first step of purifying the mind.

— Amit Ray

Quote #350

66 Altogether, the idea of meditation is not to create states of ecstasy or absorption, but to experience being.

— Chögyam Trungpa

Quote #351

66 Meditation is not evasion; it is a serene encounter with reality.

— Thích Nhất Hạnh

We are not human beings having a spiritual experience. We are spiritual beings having a human experience.

— Pierre Teilhard de Chardin

QUOTE #353

To understand the immeasurable, the mind must be extraordinarily quiet, still.

— Jiddu Krishnamurti

QUOTE #354

Inner peace begins the moment you choose not to allow another person or event to control your emotions.

— Pema Chödrön

QUOTE #355

When you realize nothing is lacking, the whole world belongs to you.

— Lao Tzu

Quote #356

66 Peace is not a passive attitude; it is an active state. It requires having constant attention in order to live without causing damage.

— Thích Nhất Hạnh

Quote #357

66 Knowing others is wisdom, knowing yourself is Enlightenment.

— Lao Tzu

Quote #358

66 Everything that has a beginning has an ending. Make your peace with that and all will be well.

— Jack Kornfield

Quote #359

66 The thing about meditation is: You become more and more you.

— David Lynch

Quote #360

66 All the powers in the universe are already ours. It is we who have put our hands before our eyes and cry that it is dark.

— Swami Vivekananda

Quote #361

66 Awakening is not changing who you are, but discarding who you are not.

— Deepak Chopra

Quote #362

66 Do not follow the ideas of others, but learn to listen to the voice within yourself.

— Zen Master Dogen

Quote #363

66 Your task is not to seek for love, but merely to seek and find all the barriers within yourself that you have built against it.

— Rumi

" The spiritual journey is the unlearning of fear and the acceptance of love.

— Marianne Williamson

QUOTE #365

" True enlightenment is nothing but the nature of one's own self being fully realized.

— Dalai Lama

~

Reflections

1. When do you feel most at peace? What activities or environments help you achieve a state of mindfulness?

_____

_____

_____

2. Reflect on a time when you felt stressed or overwhelmed. How could practicing mindfulness have helped you in that situation?

_____

_____

_____

3. How do you currently incorporate mindfulness into your daily routine? Are there additional practices you can explore?

_____

_____

_____

Practice

➤ Start a daily meditation practice, even if it's just for a few minutes. Focus on your breath and let go of any distracting thoughts.

➤ Practice mindful eating by paying full attention to the taste, texture, and sensation of each bite. Appreciate your food without distractions.

➤ Take a mindful walk in nature. Notice the sights, sounds, and smells around you, and allow yourself to be fully present in the moment.

Conclusion

As we close the pages of "365 Inspirational & Motivational Quotes to Live By," it's time to reflect on the journey we've taken together through the rich tapestry of human experience. This collection has provided you with a daily source of wisdom and encouragement, touching on various aspects of life—from overcoming adversity and personal growth to fostering relationships and achieving success. Each quote serves as a small yet powerful reminder of the resilience, creativity, and compassion that define our shared humanity.

The benefits of engaging with these quotes daily are profound. They can help shift your perspective, provide clarity in moments of doubt, and offer solace during challenging times. By integrating these insights into your everyday life, you are cultivating a mindset that embraces positivity, perseverance, and continuous growth. This book is more than just a compilation of words; it is a companion designed to support you in every phase of your journey.

We encourage you to return to these pages often. Let them be a source of daily inspiration, a wellspring of motivation, and a reminder of the incredible potential that lies within you. Whether you are facing a new challenge, seeking personal development, or simply needing a moment of reflection, these quotes will be here to guide and uplift you.

Remember, the journey of self-discovery and personal growth is ongoing. Each day offers a new opportunity to learn, to grow, and to become a better version of yourself. Use this book as a tool to harness the power of positive thinking, to strengthen your resolve, and to foster a deeper connection with yourself and others.

Thank you for allowing this book to be part of your journey. May the wisdom contained within these pages continue to inspire and motivate you, helping you to navigate life's complexities with grace and determination. Keep these words close to your heart and come back whenever you need a boost of inspiration. Here's to a life filled with resilience, joy, and boundless possibilities!

Your feedback is greatly appreciated!

It's through your feedback, support and reviews that we're able to create the best books possible and serve more people.

We would be extremely grateful if you could take just 60 seconds to kindly leave an honest review of the book on Amazon. Please share your feedback and thoughts for others to see.

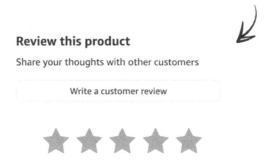

Review this product

Share your thoughts with other customers

Write a customer review

It only takes a minute to leave your mark!
Just scan the QR code below and share your thoughts:

That's it! Thank you so much for your support.

Unlock the Entrepreneurial Spirit

Exclusive Bonus Chapter Just for You!

Are you enjoying the wisdom and inspiration from *365 Inspirational & Motivational Quotes to Live By*? Dive even deeper into the journey of success with our exclusive bonus chapter, "The Entrepreneurial Spirit."

This special chapter is packed with quotes and insights from some of the world's most successful entrepreneurs and startup founders. Discover the secrets behind their incredible journeys, and gain the motivation and strategies you need to turn your own dreams into reality.

What You'll Get

- **Inspiring Quotes:** Handpicked quotes from top entrepreneurs like Elon Musk, Sara Blakely, and Richard Branson.
- **Real-Life Examples:** Learn from the triumphs and challenges of renowned business leaders.

- **Practical Reflections and Practices:** Engage with thought-provoking questions and actionable steps to ignite your entrepreneurial journey.

Don't miss out on this exclusive content designed to propel you towards your goals. Simply scan the QR code below to sign up for your FREE PDF of "The Entrepreneurial Spirit" bonus chapter.

Unlock your potential and join a community of motivated individuals ready to take on the world. Sign up today and start your journey to entrepreneurial success!

About Prosper Press

Prosper Press is a publisher dedicated to empowering individuals with the knowledge and skills they need to achieve financial freedom and personal growth. With a passion for financial literacy and personal development, we are committed to equipping our readers with the tools and insights necessary to navigate the complexities of today's financial landscape.

At Prosper Press, we recognize that everyone's financial journey is unique, which is why we offer a diverse selection of books tailored to various financial goals and learning preferences. From mastering budgeting and investing basics to unlocking the secrets of wealth creation and entrepreneurship, our collection covers a wide spectrum of topics essential for building a prosperous future.

Our approach to financial education is rooted in empowerment and positivity. We believe in fostering a mindset of abundance and possibility, inspiring readers to take control of their financial destinies with confidence and determination. By emphasizing practical strategies and actionable advice, we aim to make the journey to financial success both enriching and fulfilling.

Join us on the path to prosperity, where knowledge meets opportunity, and dreams become realities. Subscribe on our website at **ProsperPressPublishing.com** for updates and exclusive offers.